Awaken

CARMEN SANTIAGO-KEENON

WordPower Book Series

For more information, contact:

Fig Factor Media, LLC | www.figfactormedia.com

Cover Design & Layout by Juan Pablo Ruiz
Printed in the United States of America

ISBN: 978-1-959989-41-7
Library of Congress Control Number: 2023915595

DEDICATION

To Kane, Lili, and Gabriel,

This book is dedicated to you, my precious children. You are the inspiration that ignites my spirit and fills my life with immeasurable joy. Each of you holds a unique place in my heart, and it is through your love and unwavering support that I find the strength to overcome any obstacle that comes my way. May this dedication serve as a testament to the depth of my love for you and the boundless pride I feel for the incredible individuals you are becoming.

You are my insides.
Love, Mom

ACKNOWLEDGMENTS

First – To God Be the Glory for my Life. Kane, Lili, and Gabe - My insides. My world. My why.

To my abuela, Carmen Ojeda: Your love and wisdom have shaped me into the person I am today. Your strength and resilience have been my guiding light. Through your love and support, you have instilled in me the belief that anything is possible. This dedication honors the legacy of your love and the profound impact you have had on my life.

To my Heart Parents, Paul, and Jill Keenon: Your selfless devotion and belief in me have been a constant source of inspiration. Your guidance and encouragement have empowered me to pursue my dreams fearlessly. This dedication is a testament to the incredible bond we share and the profound gratitude I hold in my heart for your unconditional love.

To my Tribe: My siblings, the Hertz family, Sara, Carolyn, Lori, and Michelle, and Amy. You are the pillars of strength and the warriors who have stood by my side through thick and thin. Your unwavering support, laughter, and encouragement have lifted me up when I needed it most. This dedication is a tribute to the unbreakable bond we share, and the knowledge that I am forever blessed to have you as my chosen family.

May this book reflect the love and gratitude I hold for each of you. It is through your presence in my life that I have found the courage to overcome challenges and embrace the beauty of every moment.

To Pilotina: Thank you for inviting me on this beautiful journey of authorship.
Thank you for trusting me to be a part of your vision and for giving me a platform to share my testimony. Keep flying high!

INTRO

Awaken - The Profound Journey of Spiritual Awakening

Spiritual awakening is an intensely transformative experience that unveils the deepest layers of our existence and propels us toward a profound understanding of our purpose in life. It is a journey that transcends the boundaries of the physical realm and opens doors to a higher level of consciousness.

At its core, spiritual awakening is a personal quest for truth, a process of self-discovery, and a realization of the interconnectedness of all things. It often arises from a profound sense of discontent (for me a dark night of the soul, depression, and anxiety), urging us to seek answers beyond the materialistic pursuits of the world. Through introspection, prayer, and therapy we embark on a path of inner exploration, shedding the illusions of ego and societal conditioning, Spiritual awakening brings about a profound transformation in our perceptions, values, and behaviors. It leads us to embrace compassion, empathy, and love—not only towards others, but also towards ourselves. It awakens a heightened sense of awareness, enabling us to see beauty in the simplest of things and find purpose in every experience.

My spiritual awakening was a transformative journey. It was an invitation to dive into the depths of my being, transcend the limitations of my mind, and awaken my identity in Christ. Through this process, I discovered my interconnectedness with God and the universe. I learned to embrace love, compassion, and find meaning and purpose in my life.

My hope is that this book encourages you to reawaken yourself and discover God's love and purpose for your life.

AWAKENING THROUGH MOTHERHOOD
A JOURNEY OF TRANSFORMATION

Childbirth is often described as a sacred experience that can awaken the deepest aspects of the human spirit. It is a profound journey that can lead to a spiritual awakening unlike any other transformation.

As a new life emerges into the world, a mother taps into a strength and courage she never knew existed within her. The intensity of labor and the profound connection between mother and child creates a sacred space where the boundaries between the physical and spiritual realms blur. In this liminal space, a woman may experience a deep sense of connection to God.

Spiritual awakening during birth goes beyond the physical act of bringing new life into the world. It is a reminder of our divine nature, our capacity for love and resilience, and the interconnectedness of all beings. It is a transformative journey that invites us to embrace the profound mysteries of life and honor the sacredness inherent in every birth.

AWAKENING THROUGH LOSS: THE JOURNEY OF HEALING AND TRANSFORMATION

Loss is an inevitable part of the human experience, and within its depths lies the potential for profound awakening. Through the pain, grief, and heartache that accompany loss, we embark on a transformative journey of self-discovery and growth.

When we lose someone or something dear to us, our world is shattered. We are confronted with the fragility of life and the impermanence of our existence. It is in these moments of profound loss that we are forced to confront our deepest fears, question our beliefs, and reevaluate our priorities. As we navigate the landscape of loss, we begin to redefine our understanding of what truly matters. We learn to cherish the present moment, to cultivate gratitude for the blessings that remain, and to release the attachments that no longer serve us. Through the process of healing, we emerge with a renewed sense of purpose, a deeper appreciation for life's precious moments, and a profound understanding of our own resilience.

Awakening through loss is not an easy journey. It requires us to lean into the pain, embrace the darkness, and surrender to the process of forgiveness. However, in the depths of our sorrow, we can find solace, hope, and the potential for profound transformation. Give it to God.

AWAKENING THROUGH FALLING IN LOVE: THE POWER OF CONNECTION AND SELF-DISCOVERY

Falling in love has the remarkable ability to awaken our souls, ignite our spirits, and expand our understanding of ourselves and the world around us. It is a journey that can lead to profound personal growth and self-discovery.

When we fall in love, we open ourselves up to vulnerability and connection. We let down our guard and allow another person to see us in our raw and authentic state. In this process, we discover parts of ourselves that were previously hidden or forgotten. Love becomes a mirror, reflecting our strengths, weaknesses, desires, and fears. Love also has the potential to reveal our shadows and insecurities. It can expose our fears of abandonment or intimacy. Through this awareness, we are given the opportunity to confront and heal these wounds, cultivating personal growth and emotional resilience.

Awakening through falling in love requires openness, self-reflection, and a willingness to embrace the challenges and joys that come with it. It is a transformative journey that deepens our understanding of ourselves, our capacity to love, and to receive love. To love as God loves.

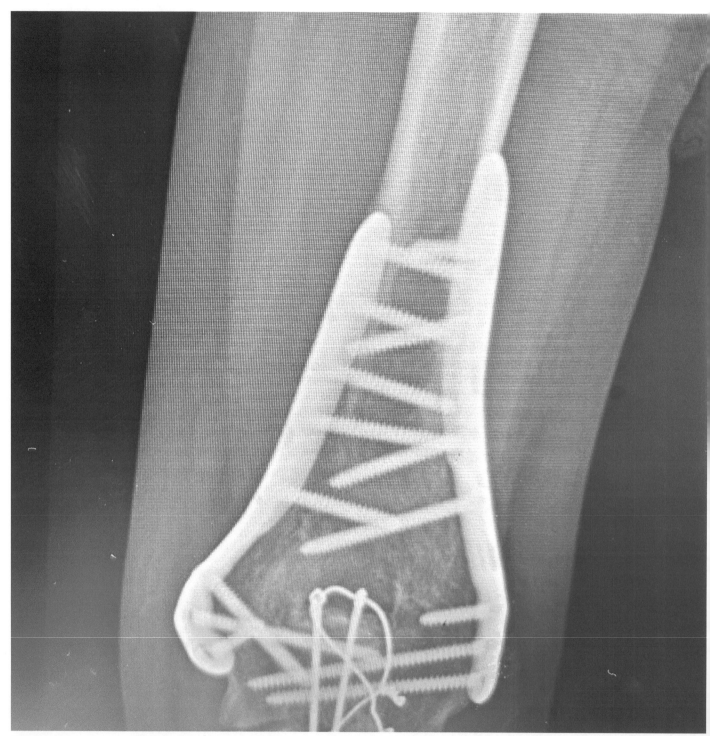

AWAKENING THROUGH BROKEN-NESS AND ABUSE: MAKING BEAUTY FROM ASHES

Awakening through brokenness and abuse is an extraordinary journey of resilience, healing, and profound forgiveness. While it may seem paradoxical, it is often in the depths of our pain and suffering that we encounter the catalysts for spiritual awakening.

Abuse and brokenness can shatter the very foundations of our being, leaving us feeling lost, fragmented, and hopeless. However, it is precisely in these darkest moments that we are compelled to seek a deeper meaning and purpose in our lives. This is how I found my faith in Jesus.

Through the process of healing and forgiveness, people who have experienced brokenness and abuse can embark on a path towards awakening. It begins with acknowledging and facing the pain, bravely confronting the wounds that have scarred the soul.

As healing unfolds, the journey of awakening emerges from the depths of forgiveness. It involves unraveling layers of hurt and confusion, conditioning, societal expectations, and distorted beliefs about self-worth. Through prayer, therapy, and support, survivors begin to reclaim their power, understand their inherent resilience, and rediscover their authentic selves.

WELCOME HOME CHILD

I peeled my face back today

I do not know what I expected to see...? the person I once had been, the person I had become or the person I intended to be.

Either way, I was a stranger to myself, staring back at me were the eyes that held stories and reflections of my past lives, forgotten pieces of myself collecting dust... and scattered throughout my souls' empty shelves.

In the depths of my being, a dormant flame, A whispering call, a voice without a name, awakening to discover what lies within, to embrace the truth. God calling me his.

Through the tangled maze of doubts and fears, my path unfolds, as clarity nears, Unveiling the layers that mask my soul.

Awakening to myself, a gentle rebirth. peeling back the layers of false pretense, Revealing my essence, raw and intense. Embracing the shadows, the light, and the gray, the flaws and scars that paved my way.

Awakening myself, a celebration of truth, A dance of authenticity, unrestrained and uncouth.

I am a symphony of emotions untold, A canvas of stories waiting to unfold.

Discovering the dreams that slumbered deep, the passions that ignite my soul's leap, awakening to my purpose, my unique art. God's grand design... I peeled my face back today...

"Life without playing music is inconceivable for me," he declared. "I live my daydreams in music. I see my life in terms of music ... I get most joy in life out of music." Elbert Einstein

AWAKENING THROUGH MUSIC:
RHYTHM OF LIFE AND THE DIVINE

Music and worship have a unique power to touch our souls, awaken dormant emotions, and elevate our consciousness. It is a universal language that transcends cultural boundaries and speaks directly to our hearts. Throughout history, music has been a catalyst for personal and collective transformation, opening doors to new perspectives, and expanding our understanding of the world.

When we listen to music or worship, we embark on a journey within ourselves. It can evoke deep emotions, stirring memories and feelings we may have long forgotten. It can transport us to various times and places, allowing us to experience the full range of human emotions. From joy and happiness to sadness and grief, music has the power to heal, comfort, and uplift. Moreover, music can awaken our inner selves, unlocking hidden potentials and revealing profound truths. It has been used as a tool for meditation and spiritual practices for centuries. Certain melodies and rhythms can induce states of deep relaxation, facilitating a connection with our higher selves and the divine. In these moments, we transcend the boundaries of our physical existence.

Whether it is the enchanting notes of a classical symphony, the soul-stirring melodies of a blues guitar, or the rhythmic beats of a conga drum, music and worship can awaken our spirits and ignite a sense of wonder and awe. It provides a gateway to explore the depths of our own being and connect with something greater than ourselves—to connect to God.

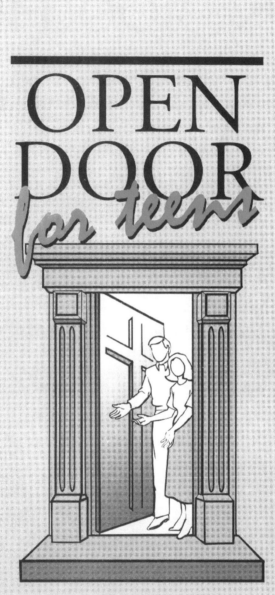

For I know the plans I have for you, declares the Lord, plans for welfare and not for calamity to give you a future and a hope.

Jeremiah 29:11

AWAKENING THROUGH RANDOM ACTS OF KINDNESS

""The most important [commandment] . . . is this: '. . . Love the Lord your God. . .' The second is this: 'Love your neighbor as yourself.'"

Mark 12:29-31

Random acts of kindness have the extraordinary power to awaken our sense of compassion and empathy. They are simple, yet profound, gestures that can transform not only the lives of others, but also our own. When we engage in acts of kindness without any expectation of reward or recognition, we open ourselves to live the way God calls us to.

By extending a helping hand to someone in need or showing a small act of kindness to a stranger, we awaken the dormant empathy within us. It reminds us that we are all connected as human beings, and our actions have the potential to create ripples of positivity in the world. Whether it is offering a smile, holding the door for someone, or lending a listening ear, these small acts have the power to brighten someone's day and make a lasting impact.

Moreover, engaging in random acts of kindness shifts our focus away from ourselves and toward the well-being of others. It helps us to break free from self-centered thinking and opens our hearts to the needs and struggles of those around us. In doing so, we become more aware of the interconnectedness of humanity, realizing that our actions, no matter how small, can make a significant difference in someone's life.

Awakening through random acts of kindness is a powerful way to connect with our higher selves and create a more compassionate world. By embracing kindness as a way of life, we awaken our sense of empathy, shift our focus away from ourselves, and experience the joy that comes from making a positive impact on others. Let us cultivate kindness in our daily lives and spread its transformative power everywhere. Love thy neighbor.

AWAKENING THROUGH LAUGHTER: EMBRACING JOY AND REDISCOVERING OUR AUTHENTIC SELVES

"Laughter is good medicine."

Proverbs 17:22.

Awakening through laughter is a process of rediscovering the joy and playfulness that may have become buried beneath the responsibilities and challenges of adulthood. It reminds me to not take life too seriously and find moments of levity even in chaos.

In the presence of laughter, we connect with others on a deep and genuine level. Laughter is a universal language that transcends cultural boundaries and brings people together. It fosters a sense of belonging and community, creating bonds that enrich our lives and provide support during tough times.

Furthermore, laughter is a powerful tool for self-healing and emotional well-being. It releases endorphins, reduces stress, and boosts our immune system. Laughing allows us to release pent-up emotions and find catharsis, promoting a greater sense of inner peace and harmony.

Awakening through laughter is a transformative experience that rejuvenates our spirits, renews our perspective, and reconnects us with our authentic selves. Through laughter, we tap into the essence of joy and cultivate a greater appreciation for life's simplest pleasures. So let us embrace laughter, cherish its transformative power, and allow it to guide us on a journey of self-discovery, connection, and unbridled joy.

AWAKENING THROUGH FORGIVENESS:
UNTANGLING THE MESS OF OFFENSE

""Let all bitterness and wrath and anger and clamor and slander be put away from you, along with all malice. Be kind to one another, tenderhearted, forgiving one another, as God in Christ forgave you."

Ephesians 4:31-32

Forgiveness is a profound act that has the power to liberate us from the burdens of resentment, anger, and pain. It is a transformative process that allows us to awaken to our true selves, promoting healing, growth, and inner peace.

Forgiveness does not mean condoning or forgetting the wrongs done to us. It is a conscious choice to release the negative emotions and the desire for revenge or retribution. It is an act of compassion towards us and others, a recognition of our shared humanity and vulnerability. The way of the cross.

Forgiveness allows us to break free from the past and live in the present moment. It liberates us from the shackles of resentment and bitterness, allowing us to embrace the fullness of life with a new understanding and renewal of the mind.

Let us learn to embrace the power of forgiveness and experience the freedom and inner peace it brings.

DRY BONES AWAKEN!!!

I am on my knees singing out into this land.... Dry Bones Awaken!!!

In the barren depths where life has waned, where hope has withered, and dreams have strained,

A whisper echoes through the vast unknown, A call to awaken the dry bones.

In the desert of despair, they lay still, Devoid of vigor, devoid of will, but a spark ignites within the core, Breathing life into bones, forevermore.

From the ashes of desolation and dust, A symphony rises, a melody robust, the rhythm of revival begins to play, As the dry bones dance in the light of day.

With every step, the ground trembles, and shakes, As the bones arise, like an army, awake, their spirits rekindled, their hearts beating anew, From a state of stagnation, to vibrant and true.

In this dance of resurrection, they find their voice, singing a song of triumph, a chorus of choice, No longer bound by the chains of the past, they embrace the future, with strength unsurpassed.

Awakening from slumber, they soar to the skies, with wings unfurled, reaching new highs, no longer confined by what once held them down, they rise above, where hope knows no bounds.

Awakening dry bones, a testament profound, that even in darkness, life can be found, with resilience and spirit, they break through the mold, for even the driest bones can be awakened and bold...

Dry Bones Come alive through life in Christ, the way truth and life

Awaken the part
of your soul that
wants to catch
the sun and dance
with the ocean

start now!

CSK

CONCLUSION

In conclusion, spiritual awakening, coupled with a growth mindset, unlocks the extraordinary potential within us, enabling us to embark on a transformative journey of self-discovery and personal growth. Just as the sun rises each day, symbolizing new beginnings, we, too, have the power to catch its radiant rays and infuse our lives with purpose and meaning. By embracing a growth mindset, we embrace the notion that our abilities and intelligence are not fixed, but rather can be developed through dedication and effort. This mindset fuels our spiritual awakening, propelling us forward on a path of continuous learning and expansion.

As we dance with the ocean, we surrender ourselves to the ebb and flow of life, embracing both its gentle waves and turbulent currents. Through this dance, we cultivate resilience, adaptability, and a deep understanding of our interconnectedness with the world around us. Spiritual awakening with a growth mindset invites us to let go of limiting beliefs and embrace the infinite possibilities that await us. With every step we take, we become more attuned to our true selves and the profound wisdom that lies within. So, let us catch the sun, dance with the ocean, and embark on this wondrous journey of spiritual awakening, forever evolving, and radiating our inner light for all to see.

Now that your eyes are open, make the sun jealous with your burning passion to start the day. Make the sun jealous or stay in bed.

MALAK EL HALABI

Creating a routine for an Awakening journal can be a powerful practice to deepen your spiritual journey and foster self-discovery. Here's a suggested routine to incorporate into your Co-creating with God practice:

1. Set a Sacred Space: Find a quiet and peaceful place where you can journal without distractions. Light a candle or burn incense to create a sacred ambiance.

2. Begin with Gratitude: Start your journaling session by expressing gratitude. Write down three things you are grateful for, acknowledging the blessings and abundance in your life.

3. Reflect on the Previous Day: Take a few moments to reflect on the events, experiences, and emotions of the previous day. Write about any insights or lessons you gained, moments of joy or challenges, and how they align with your spiritual journey.

4. Set an Intention: Set an intention for the day ahead. What aspect of your spiritual awakening would you like to focus on or cultivate? Write a clear and concise I CHOOSE intention statement.

5. Dive into Self-Reflection: Pose thought-provoking questions to explore your inner self. Examples could include: "What limiting beliefs am I ready to release?", "What patterns or habits no longer serve my spiritual growth?", or "What brings me closer to my true essence?"

6. Closing Meditation or Prayer: Close your journaling session with a short meditation or prayer. Center yourself, express gratitude for the insights gained, and invite guidance and wisdom on your continued spiritual journey.

Remember, this routine is flexible, and you can modify it to suit your preferences and needs. The goal is to create a space for self-reflection, introspection, and connection with your inner wisdom as you navigate the path of awakening.

ABOUT THE AUTHOR

Carmen Santiago-Keenon's journey from a foster child to CEO, community activist, STEAM enthusiast, and focus on human-centered work is a testament to the human spirit's resilience. Through determination, hard work, and an unwavering belief in herself, she overcame countless obstacles and forged her own path toward success. Today, Carmen stands as an inspiration to aspiring STEAM students and individuals who dare to dream big. Her story serves as a  reminder that, regardless of our circumstances, we all possess the power to rise above and create a better future for ourselves and choose to AWAKEN and actively participate in creating our lives.

Beyond her professional pursuits and philanthropic endeavors, Carmen finds solace in her personal life. She cherishes her role as a mother to three incredible children: Kane, Lili, and Gabe. Alongside her children, Carmen shares her home with two mischievous cats, Prince Charles, and Bean, who bring endless laughter and love to their lives. In her spare time, she indulges in her passion for music, playing her congas and singing, creating a sense of balance and fulfillment.

CONTACT:
Facebook: Carmen Santiago-Keenon
LinkedIn: Carmen Santiago-Keenon
www.itgirlsolutions.com

HOW DOES THE WORD **AWAKEN** EMPOWER YOU?